TO YOU, AN UNSTOPPABLE DREAMER
AND CREATOR, WHO HAS THE POWER
TO IMPROVE THE WORLD.

WE BELIEVE IN YOU!

GET IN TOUCH

hello@biglifejournal.com

LEARN MORE
www.biglifejournal.com

Printed in Canada

Published by Eidens, Inc.

THIS JOURNAL BELONGS TO

WHAT DO YOU DREAM OF BECOMING?

Really. Have you thought about it? Perhaps, you have and you already have a clear vision. Or maybe you haven't, which is okay too.

The reality is when you do think about these things (what you want to be/do/accomplish) you're much more likely to live the life you want to live - your dream life. You're much more likely to have great friendships and relationships, do what you want to do, go to places you want to go, have things you want to have.

It just takes a bit of dreaming, planning, and even writing things down. And then, of course, doing those things.

And there's one thing which can help you BIG time. It's your mindset. You see, your mind is very powerful. The way you think about yourself and the world around you can make a huge difference as to whether or not you get to where you want to go.

So take a chance... complete this journal. Take time to dream and think about your life now and in the future. It can be as wild and adventurous, or as calm and quiet, as you want it to be - it's up to you.

So, whether you have a clear vision already, or haven't visualized the great things you'll do in life, where you are right now is the perfect place to start.

WHAT'S IN THIS JOURNAL?

This journal is broken down into five chapters. They're designed to be completed in this sequence, however, use it the way it works for you.

CHAPTER 1 – IT ALL STARTS HERE   6
You will discover the power of your mind and learn about different types of mindset.

CHAPTER 2 – EXPLORING YOU   34
You will do some fun activities to discover your true interests.

CHAPTER 3 – DREAMING UP YOUR LIFE   68
This is where you can have your imagination run completely free as you're dreaming about your future and your ideal life.

CHAPTER 4 – FROM DREAMS TO REALITY   96
You will discover tools and tips on how to turn your dreams into reality.

CHAPTER 5 – THE KEY TO SUCCESS   128
This one is very important! You will learn how to persist through challenges and difficult times in order to reach your goals.

Let the journey begin!

IT ALL STARTS HERE!

Everything in life starts with your mindset.
Your mindset is how you think about yourself
and the world around you. It is the foundation
of your success and happiness!

A positive mindset can help you become
successful, confident, and live a big life.
A negative mindset can prevent you from
reaching your goals and make you miserable.

Remember, you can always change your mindset!

Whether you think you can or think you can't you are Right

Henry Ford

HAVE you ever thought "I am not good enough" or "I will never be able to do this"?

These types of thoughts usually make us feel unmotivated, defeated, and stressed. It's perfectly normal to think this way sometimes. However, when we think this way most of the time, these thoughts can prevent us from creating the life we want.

Research shows successful people have other types of thoughts more often. If you were to get inside their minds, you would hear something like, "I can accomplish anything!" and "I love this challenge!"

THESE TYPES OF THOUGHTS FORM A POSITIVE MINDSET AND MAKE US SUCCESSFUL.

By thinking this way, we form strong positive beliefs about ourselves which help us reach our dreams and make us unstoppable!

So let's see what kind of thoughts flow around in your head most often. On a scale of 1 – 5, with 1 being "you don't agree" and 5 being "you strongly agree", score yourself.

You generally say negative things about yourself.

1   2   3   4   (5)

You have a hard time finding positive things in most situations.

1   2   (3)   4   5

You think your current lifestyle will limit your success.

(1)   2   3   4   5

There's nothing exciting to look forward to in the future.

1   (2)   3   4   5

You believe you can't really change how intelligent you are.

1   2   3   (4)   5

Now add up your numbers above and see where you score below.

5 - 10 You've got a pretty positive mindset!

11 - 20 Your thoughts and your mindset might be holding you back.

21 - 25 Your negative thoughts really bring you down.

It's natural and healthy to experience a wide range of thoughts and feelings, including less pleasant ones like disappointment, sadness, or guilt. There are no wrong thoughts - some thoughts just don't serve you as well as others.

YOU CAN LIVE THE LIFE OF YOUR DREAMS BY...

REWIRING YOUR BRAIN

Your brain is VERY POWERFUL! You can rewire your brain with your thoughts and experiences so that it can help you LIVE THE LIFE YOU WANT.

GREATER ACHIEVEMENTS

POSITIVE FRIENDSHIPS AND RELATIONSHIPS

DREAM CAREER

...AND EVEN STRONGER BODY

HOW?

The human brain has the amazing ability to change and adapt by forming and eliminating connections between its cells (NEURONS).

Establishing new neural connections between brain cells is like building a bridge to cross a ravine.

The first time you cross the ravine, it requires a lot of effort. The first trip is the hardest.

Having crossed the ravine once, the journey across gets easier & easier.

You begin building a bridge across the ravine, which will make it very easy for you to cross it in the future.

Similarly, when you think a repetitive thought or practice something over and over, your brain is building and strengthening new bridges.

You can decide which bridges you want to:

BUILD & WHICH TO TEAR DOWN

YOUR BRAIN IS A SUPERCOMPUTER AND YOUR SELF-TALK IS THE PROGRAM IT WILL RUN

JIM KWIK

Your brain, your body, and your mindset are heavily influenced by the quality of your self-talk. The things you say to yourself, and how you feel about yourself, have a big impact and are incredibly powerful.

Positive self-talk is kind, supportive, and affirming. It sounds like this "I'm making progress" or "I will keep trying"

POSITIVE SELF-TALK
boosts confidence
helps you succeed in sports
helps achieve goals
gets you through challenging times

Negative self-talk is unkind, critical, and upsetting. It can sound like "I am not worth it" or "My opinion doesn't matter"

NEGATIVE SELF-TALK
lowers self-esteem
spoils true friendships
stops you from achieving goals
increases stress

Our repetitive thoughts and self-talk form our beliefs and mindset. For example, a person may think their intelligence, talents, and abilities CAN'T be significantly improved. Researchers call this way of thinking a FIXED mindset.

I'm not a math person.

My intelligence, talents, & abilities are fixed.

I'm not a natural athlete.

I'm not good enough.

I'm not creative.

FIXED MINDSET

WE ALREADY KNOW ABOUT THE INCREDIBLE POWER OF OUR BRAIN TO LEARN AND CHANGE!

An alternative way of thinking is our intelligence, talents, and abilities CAN be developed with effort, right strategies, help from others, etc. Researchers call this way of thinking a GROWTH mindset.

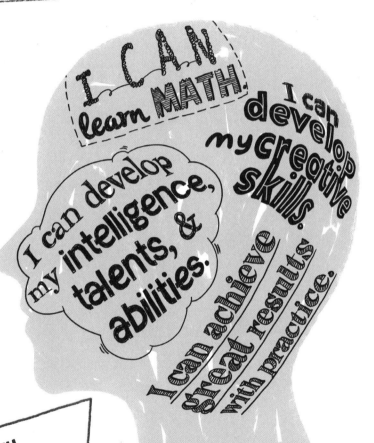

SO THE GROWTH MINDSET WAY OF THINKING IS A BETTER REFLECTION OF REALITY.

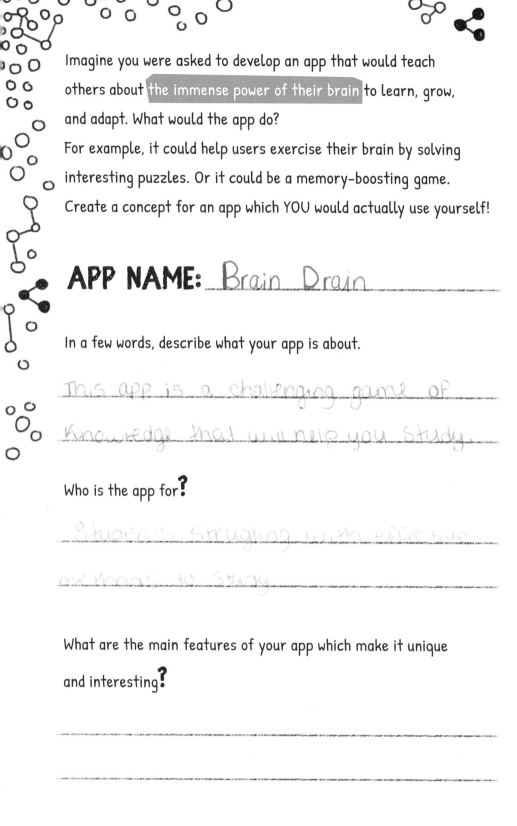

Imagine you were asked to develop an app that would teach others about the immense power of their brain to learn, grow, and adapt. What would the app do?

For example, it could help users exercise their brain by solving interesting puzzles. Or it could be a memory-boosting game. Create a concept for an app which YOU would actually use yourself!

APP NAME: Brain Drain

In a few words, describe what your app is about.

This app is a challenging game of knowledge that will help you study.

Who is the app for?

Students struggling with effective methods to study

What are the main features of your app which make it unique and interesting?

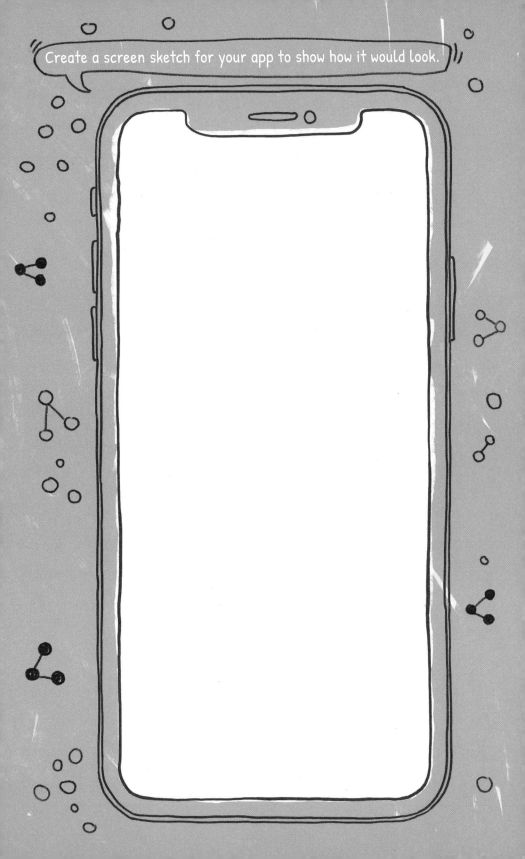

I RAN FOR A YEAR. MY ONLY GOAL WAS TO KEEP RUNNING.

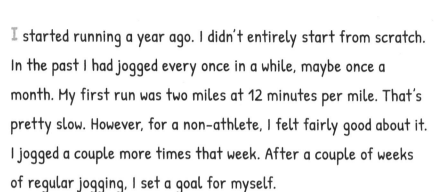

I started running a year ago. I didn't entirely start from scratch. In the past I had jogged every once in a while, maybe once a month. My first run was two miles at 12 minutes per mile. That's pretty slow. However, for a non-athlete, I felt fairly good about it. I jogged a couple more times that week. After a couple of weeks of regular jogging, I set a goal for myself.

I knew I would never be fast enough to impress anybody so it didn't make sense to make speed my goal. I could have picked a race to train for, a 5k or half miler, but I knew how those ended. Everyone seems to quit running right after their big race. I wanted to do something different. I wanted to not quit.

My goal involved not going too long between runs. If I skipped more than a couple of days, wouldn't that be quitting? So I started running four - five days a week. The longest I went between runs was three days when I was on vacation in Hawaii.

My goal made all the difference. I was still slow, but I felt good about running a lot. I'd have good days where I would run fast and feel great but I also had lots of bad days where I was tired and just didn't feel like running. In retrospect, those days were almost better than the good days because they reinforced my goal — I didn't quit.

I ran my first 5k on Halloween, nearly five months after I had taken up running as a hobby. I wore a costume — fairy wings — and tried to keep up with a random guy with an owl on his head. I finished in 28 minutes and was super happy. I learned racing wasn't always about being the fastest, but doing my personal best.

I signed up to run a full marathon in December, hired a running coach, and set a regular running schedule. I've started to think of myself as a runner. If you would have told me a year ago that I would be working out almost every day and running 100 miles a month, I would never have believed you. Running really snuck up on me. I had modest aspirations and didn't really care if I was great at running. I just wanted to stick to my one goal: don't quit.

LEAH CULVER   startup founder

Leah Culver started as a slow and inexperienced runner (she was a startup founder, after all, not a professional athlete).

She knew she could improve as long as she stayed consistent and didn't quit. So, she focused on the process and on showing up.

By having a growth mindset about running, sticking to the schedule, and "not quitting", she was able to reach extraordinary results.

It is common to have a growth mindset in one area and a fixed mindset in another. For example, a runner who knows she CAN improve her marathon time with practice (growth mindset), might think she is terrible at building relationships (fixed mindset). Mark the scale where you think your mindset falls in the areas listed below.

WHEN I THINK ABOUT MY:	MY MINDSET IS MOSTLY
	FIXED ———————————— GROWTH
ABILITY TO CONCENTRATE	
FRIENDSHIPS / RELATIONSHIPS	
READING ABILITIES	
WRITING ABILITIES	
MATH ABILITIES	
OVERALL ACADEMIC POTENTIAL	
PERFORMANCE IN SPORTS	
BODY IMAGE AND LOOKS	
CHARACTER	
ARTISTIC SKILLS	

HAVE YOU USED AFFIRMATIONS?

An effective way to shut down your negative self-talk is to use positive affirmations. It's a common strategy used by some of the most successful people in the world. And like most things you practice, the more you do it, the easier and more effective it becomes!

PRO TIPS:

1. Speak in the present (be Yoda, not Luke)

2. Don't speak in absolutes ("always" and "never")

3. Keep it simple (use short, powerful sentences)

4. Make it real (say it out loud, stand up, gesture too!)

5. Visualize your statement (athletes do it)

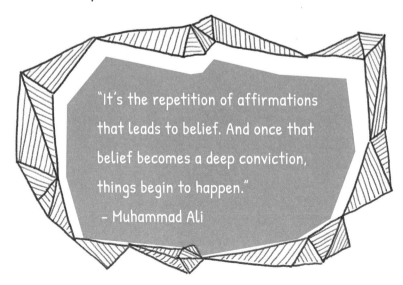

"It's the repetition of affirmations that leads to belief. And once that belief becomes a deep conviction, things begin to happen."
- Muhammad Ali

PICTURE this: in a sport where fists do the talking and silent masculinity reigns, a man with a quick wit, poetic gift, and exuberant confidence thought his way to success. He was born Cassius Clay and transformed himself into MUHAMMAD ALI, the greatest boxer in history. He was not the strongest, he was not the biggest, but he was the best. How do we know? Because he said so!

He began with a thought, repeated it, and let belief follow after. "I figured that if I said it enough, I would convince the world that I really was the greatest." This belief seeped through his bones and began to transform his actions, his abilities...his future. Ali showed us ability is one thing, but self-belief and positive thoughts are the difference between good and great.

I LEARN FROM FAILURES I AM ARTISTIC I AM CAPABLE

FUNNY I LOVE LEARNING

POSITIVE STRONG

I WORK HARD My IDEAS Are UNIQUE

I DON'T GIVE UP I TRAIN MY BRAIN

I AM RESILIENT

I BELIEVE IN ME THOUGHTFUL

INSIGHTFUL I CAN ACHIEVE GREAT THINGS

I CAN ALWAYS IMPROVE I CHEER MYSELF UP I GO AFTER MY DREAMS

I DO MY BEST GRATEFUL LOVED & LOVING

CARING

CREATIVE RESOURCEFUL I AM A PROBLEM SOLVER

UNSTOPPABLE

AMBITIOUS I PRACTICE TO GET BETTER

I TRY NEW THINGS I AM BRAVE FOR TRYING

Practice creating positive affirmations for yourself. Complete the sentences below and write your own in the empty spaces. If you get stuck, look at the previous page for inspiration.

I CAN

I LOVE

I BELIEVE

I AM GOOD AT

I AM

Choose one of the positive statements you wrote on the previous page and make it your mantra (a mantra is a statement you repeat frequently). Keep repeating it over and over again until you truly believe it.

It may be difficult at first, but remember, you're building a NEW bridge between brain cells, so repetition is important!

Write your positivity mantra here:

Draw or design your positivity mantra. Make it a comic, a meme, a t-shirt design, a tattoo, or anything else you'd like.

HAVE YOU EVER WONDERED WHY YOU HAVE NEGATIVE SELF-TALK IN THE FIRST PLACE?

Most beliefs are acquired from the world around you: people you spend the most time with, movies and videos you watch, music you listen to, etc.

The messages you constantly receive from outside get hardwired in your brain and become your beliefs.

YOUR THINKING IS HEAVILY INFLUENCED BY THE FIVE PEOPLE AND THINGS YOU SPEND THE MOST TIME AROUND.

Write down people and things (e.g., video games, social apps) you spend the most time with.

Mark on each scale whether the messages you receive from them are mostly negative (e.g., complaining, gossip) or positive (e.g., encouragement, love).

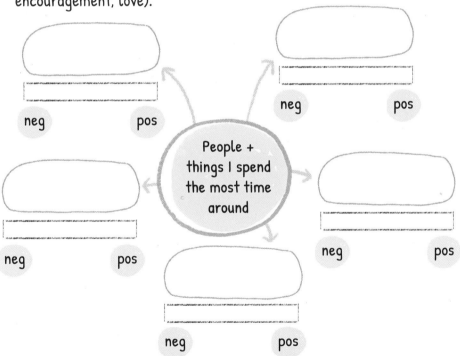

We can't always avoid people who complain or bring us down. However, we can seek out people who are supportive and uplifting and make a conscious effort to be around them more often.

HAVING A GREAT MENTOR CAN MAKE ALL THE DIFFERENCE

A mentor can help you answer a difficult question. He/she can give advice about a tough situation, help you when you're stuck, stressed, lost, or just need someone to talk to.

A GREAT MENTOR IS SOMEONE WHO...

CHALLENGES YOU

HAS A POSITIVE MINDSET

RESPECTS YOU   IS MORE EXPERIENCED

GUIDES YOU TO FIND ANSWERS

IS AVAILABLE

PROVIDES CONSTRUCTIVE FEEDBACK

CHEERS FOR YOUR SUCCESS

IS SUPPORTIVE

WHO COULD BE YOUR MENTOR?

Write down the names of people who you admire and look up to. These could be people in your life or an expert you follow on social media.

WHY DO YOU LOOK UP TO THEM?

IF YOU COULD ASK THEM ANY QUESTION, WHAT WOULD IT BE?

SIDESTEP

Create a playlist for your life.

Draw or sketch the cover to your playlist.

EXPLORING YOU

Discovering your interests and what you enjoy doing is a lifelong process and it pays off in a big way!

Start with things you're curious about. Think about what you love doing the most. You can also imagine various jobs you want to try or think about the world issues you want to work on.

Then dive into your interests and explore them further.

Knowing and developing your interests will help you set goals and dream of the life you want to have.

Not all those who wander are lost.

J. R. R. Tolkien
Author of "The Lord of the Rings"

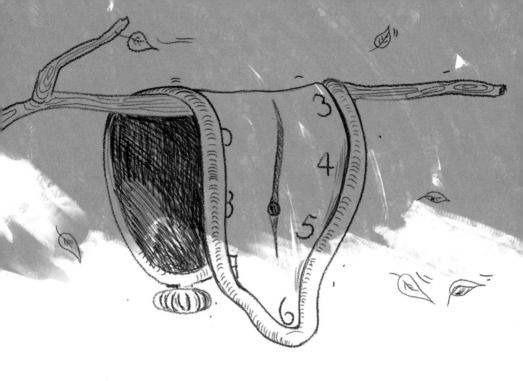

Have you ever spent what seemed like half an hour in great conversation with someone, only to realise three hours had actually passed? Or have you ever opened a book shortly after breakfast and a little while later noticed the room was getting darker?

In those moments, we are doing something we love just for the sake of doing it rather than focusing on the end result. We become so absorbed in what we're doing, nothing else seems to matter. We lose track of time and enter the state of flow. Some people call it being in the zone.

Those moments have potential to make our lives richer, more intense and more meaningful. By noticing these moments, you can discover a lot about yourself and your interests.

Describe or draw something you did recently that made you lose track of time. It could have been reading an intriguing book or blog, being part of a super interesting event, or making creative videos...

THERE ARE SO MANY WONDERFUL UNIQUE THINGS ABOUT YOU. YOU JUST NEED TO FIND THEM.

"**YOU** have to be unique and different and shine in your own way."
The person who gave the world these words knows how to practice what she preaches. LADY GAGA creates her art from her own individual uniqueness and has never tried to fit in with those around her. She not only embraces herself but she urges others to do the same. She understands being different is a gift - it's a wonderful thing. Imagine if she had compared herself to other artists and decided not to take those incredible risks with her art? Imagine if she had blended into the crowd? We wouldn't have the wild, inspiring, embracing, and encouraging role model we have now. Imagine if you blended in, too. We wouldn't have the real you. And there's only one you.

Who you are is 150% good enough. In fact, it's amazing. Even if you feel like you walk a different path than others... embrace it! You're an adventurer in your own life, so never feel like you have to follow someone else's map. Your uniqueness is your greatest gift. Show it, love it, share it. Make Lady Gaga proud.

I HAVE NO
SPECIAL TALENT.
I AM ONLY
PASSIONATELY
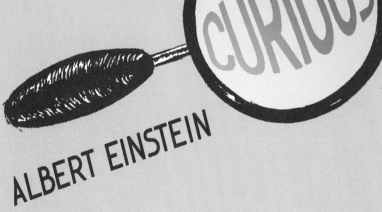
CURIOUS

ALBERT EINSTEIN

You can learn a lot about yourself by paying attention to what you're curious about: medicine, art, coding, vlogging, robotics, or anything else. Write all the things you're curious about below.

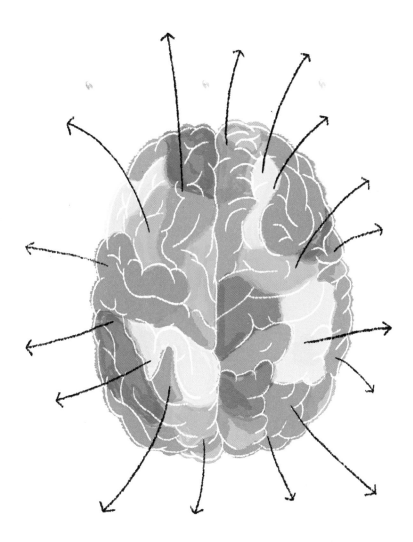

What do you enjoy DOING the most? Is it creating art, doing projects with other people, or perhaps writing?

Circle below what you like to do.

INSPIRE ENTERTAIN LEAD

RESEARCH HELP

DECORATE BUILD TALK

READ TRAVEL COMPETE

ORGANIZE

EXCEL AMAZE WRITE

LEARN LISTEN

WIN DANCE

EXPRESS PLAY ENCOURAGE

PLAN ACHIEVE

CONNECT CREATE DRAW IMPACT

TEACH

CHALLENGE PERFORM

DOODLE GIVE

COLLABORATE SING EXPLORE

Now, write down all the words you circled on the previous page and include your own which are not listed. For example, "**I LIKE TO INSPIRE, CREATE, CONNECT, AND IMPACT.**"

I LIKE TO...

CAN YOU FIND ANY PATTERNS?

Take a look at the previous page. Are there any patterns in the things you enjoy doing?

For example, you might like doing things which involve other people (e.g., entertain, inspire, give), or maybe you prefer doing things by yourself (e.g., sing, read, learn).

Or, perhaps you enjoy doing something with your hands, such as building and creating.

If you're unsure about patterns, ask someone else to take a look at your list and help you find yours.

CHECK THE BOXES BELOW FOR THE PATTERNS YOU SEE.

☐ I LIKE DOING THINGS WITH OTHER PEOPLE (E.G., COLLABORATE, TEACH).

☐ I PREFER DOING THINGS BY MYSELF (E.G., RESEARCH, READ).

☐ I LIKE CREATING THINGS WITH MY HANDS (E.G., BUILD, DRAW).

☐ I LIKE CHALLENGING ACTIVITIES AND REACHING HIGH STANDARDS (E.G., EXCEL, ACHIEVE).

☐ I ENJOY LEARNING ABOUT THE WORLD (E.G., TRAVEL, EXPLORE).

What other patterns have you noticed about what you enjoy doing?

_____

_____

_____

Sometimes we become passionate about **WORLD ISSUES** and want to do something about them.

Think about particular world issues you are interested in supporting or those in which you'd like to make a difference.

It could be anything from the lack of healthy food options to bullying, human rights, violence, destruction of nature, or unequal access to opportunities. Can you think of others?

TO GET SOME IDEAS GOING, MARK BELOW HOW MUCH YOU CARE ABOUT THE FOLLOWING WORLD ISSUES.

	don't care	care somewhat	care deeply
ANIMAL RIGHTS			
BULLYING			
GLOBAL HUNGER/ MALNUTRITION			
CRIME AND VIOLENCE			
POLLUTION			
CLIMATE CHANGE			
POVERTY			
HUMAN RIGHTS			

Are there any other causes you care deeply about and want to make a difference?

If you don't know yet, that's OK. Get inspired by passionate young people just like you! Read the incredible story of Jessica O. Matthews on the next page. Learn how she used her knowledge in physics (kinetic energy and motion) to create an awesome invention!

THINK of all the wonderful, lifesaving items we use every day... asthma medication, seatbelts, cell phones. At some point, someone realized we needed these things, even if they didn't know how to create them yet. They knew a solution existed. They kept searching until they had that "lightbulb" moment and discovered the breakthrough solution.

They studied, trained, harnessed the help of others, and worked long hours until the wheels began to turn. But all the work was worth it, as it meant something to them.

YOU can do this, too. Just look at **JESSICA O. MATTHEWS**. At only 22 she had founded Unchartered Play (later renamed Unchartered Power), which provides safe and sustainable power to people in Africa. Her lightbulb moment came while at her Aunt's wedding in Nigeria.

The power cut out and had to be restarted using diesel generators...neither a safe nor a practical solution. There had to be another way! And Jessica found it. She thought of a renewable energy soccer ball which charges up as users play. She called this ball SOCCKET and this was her very first product.

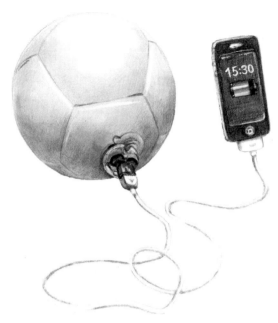

The mechanism inside the SOCCKET captures the kinetic energy generated during normal play, and stores it in the ball for later use as a power source.

Now Jessica's company has a series of incredible products which turn everyday motion into sources of power, such as energy-harnessing shopping carts and walkways.

"I always wanted to make really cool meaningful things..."

Those are Jessica's own, relatable words. Cool meaningful things. That's what life is about, isn't it? Making the world a better, more meaningful place for those around us.

Decide what would make your world better, find the solution, call on your skills, and create the change.

YOUR INTEREST IN ONE THING CAN LEAD YOU TO SOMETHING ELSE!

ONCE YOU DISCOVER THINGS YOU'RE INTERESTED IN, YOU CAN EXPLORE THOSE INTERESTS FURTHER. THAT MIGHT LEAD YOU TO MORE FASCINATING ACTIVITIES AND SUBJECTS.

HERE ARE SOME EXAMPLES:

⭐ Your interest in DRAWING may lead you to graphic design, comic book illustrations, or fashion design.

⭐ Your interest in TALKING may lead you to community management, hosting a talk show, or teaching.

⭐ Your interest in SPORTS may lead you to coaching, becoming an Olympian, or opening your own gym.

INTEREST MAPS

Interest map centered on **DRAWING** with connected bubbles: STORY-BOARDING, COMIC BOOKS, MEDICAL ILLUSTRATION, ILLUSTRATION, GRAPHIC NOVELS, FILM AND VIDEO EDITING, FASHION DESIGN, GRAPHIC DESIGN.

Interest map centered on **GIVING ADVICE** with connected bubbles: IMAGE CONSULTING, COUNSELING, CONSULTING, BUSINESS CONSULTING, COACHING, SPEAKING PUBLICLY, TEACHING.

Now create your own interest map. Choose one of your interests or a topic you're curious about. Write it down in the center circle below.

Then do the research to find related fields you can explore further. Write them down inside other circles. Add new circles if needed.

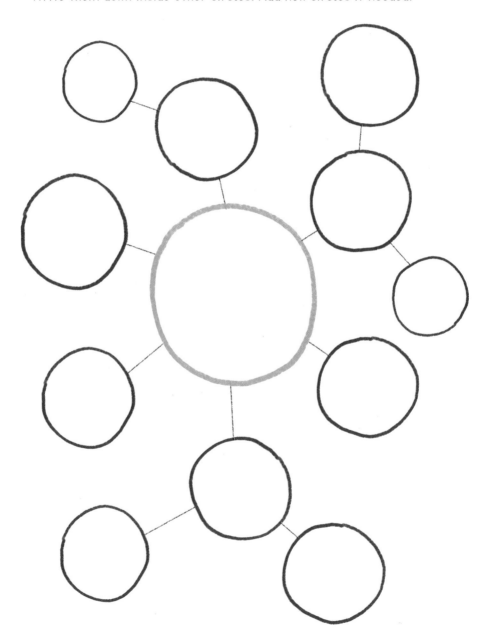

YOUR WORK IS GOING TO FILL A LARGE PART OF YOUR LIFE, AND THE ONLY WAY TO BE TRULY SATISFIED IS TO DO WHAT YOU BELIEVE IS GREAT WORK. AND THE ONLY WAY TO DO GREAT WORK IS TO LOVE WHAT YOU DO. IF YOU HAVEN'T FOUND IT YET, KEEP LOOKING. DON'T SETTLE. AS WITH ALL MATTERS OF THE HEART, YOU'LL KNOW WHEN YOU FIND IT.

STEVE JOBS
CO-FOUNDER OF APPLE

When you **TRY LOTS OF DIFFERENT ACTIVITIES**, you learn about what you like and what you don't like doing. That knowledge is important for you to find an interesting and rewarding path in life.

IMAGINE YOU COULD TRY ANY 5 JOBS FOR THREE MONTHS EACH. YOU COULD BE...

FIVE JOBS
I WOULD LIKE
TO TRY

 1

 2

 3

 4

 5

Do any of these jobs stand out in particular?

CIRCLE THE ONE
WHICH SOUNDS
THE MOST INTERESTING.

A GREAT WAY TO DISCOVER MORE ABOUT YOURSELF IS TO ASK OTHERS. FOR EXAMPLE, YOU CAN INTERVIEW PEOPLE WHO KNOW YOU BEST AND ASK THEM QUESTIONS ABOUT YOURSELF.

Write down the names of the people who know you well.

Circle two names of people you will interview and ask them the questions below. Have a face-to-face conversation, if possible.

What are my two greatest strengths ?

If I had my own show, what would it be about ?

What do you see me doing 10 years from now ?

Write your own questions:

1.

2.

3.

MY FIRST INTERVIEW

WHAT ARE MY TWO GREATEST STRENGTHS?

_____

_____

IF I HAD MY OWN SHOW, WHAT WOULD IT BE ABOUT?

_____

WHAT DO YOU SEE ME DOING 10 YEARS FROM NOW?

_____

_____

MY QUESTIONS:

1. _____

2. _____

3. _____

MY SECOND INTERVIEW

WHAT ARE MY TWO GREATEST STRENGTHS?

_____

_____

IF I HAD MY OWN SHOW, WHAT WOULD IT BE ABOUT?

_____

WHAT DO YOU SEE ME DOING 10 YEARS FROM NOW?

_____

_____

MY QUESTIONS:

1. _____

2. _____

3. _____

YOU can take something you're passionate about and turn it into a project or a business that could improve the world!

Take a look at PETE CEGLINSKI. A surfer from Australia with a deep love for the ocean and the determination to make a difference, Pete was shocked at the level of rubbish polluting our oceans.

So, with the help of his business partner, he put his thinking cap on and came up with a solution. But what he created might shock you with its simplicity and common-sense design.

Pete created the Seabin, and it's exactly how it sounds. A rubbish bin for the sea which uses a pump to draw water into the bin, trapping rubbish, and letting clean water filter through.

While his idea was simple, his journey toward success was not. It took Pete two long years to use his crowdfunding money to make

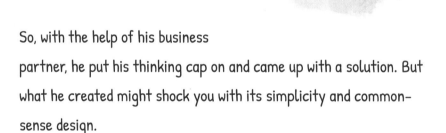

the Seabin the best, and most effective it could be, before
releasing it for presales.

Pete never gave up. He never thought his idea was too simple. He kept
going and created a product which can, does, and will continue to help
our oceans.

Take heed of what Pete Ceglinski said, "We all have the power to make
a difference." All of us. Sometimes the solution is right in front of you;
you just need to open your mind to find it. Once you do, grasp it with
both hands, don't let go, and persevere until you succeed.

HOW THE SEABIN WORKS

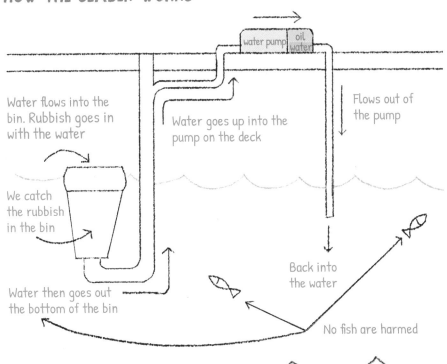

HAVE YOU EVER THOUGHT ABOUT CREATING A YOUTUBE CHANNEL?

Having a YouTube channel is a great way to explore and share your interests and passions with the world.

If you had your own video show, what would it be about?

Create a name, decide on the subject and type, and make a list of your first 3 videos.

CHANNEL NAME _____

WHAT IS IT ABOUT? _____

_____

CHANNEL TYPE (check one or more)

☐ How-to videos   ☐ Creative videos
☐ Comedy   (documentary, TV-style shows, etc.)
☐ Music videos   ☐ Vlogging

NAME YOUR FIRST 3 VIDEOS

1:

2:

3:

Every YouTube star needs a professional banner that matches the style of their channel. Use the templates to draw two variations of your channel banner. Try different styles (clean, busy, bold, etc.) and colors.

SUBSCRIBE

GO AHEAD AND RECORD YOUR FIRST VIDEO!

BASIC THINGS YOU NEED:

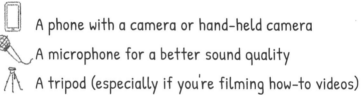

- A phone with a camera or hand-held camera
- A microphone for a better sound quality
- A tripod (especially if you're filming how-to videos)
- A simple video editing program for postproduction, particularly if you're going to include music (you could use free programs such as Microsoft Movie Maker or iMovie)

You might need additional equipment or programs depending on your channel type.

Plan out your first video here.

1. WHAT WILL IT BE ABOUT?

2. DECIDE ON THE LENGTH OF THE VIDEO

3. SELECT MUSIC YOU WILL USE

4. WRITE AN OUTLINE FOR YOUR VIDEO
(what you will say and show)

5. GATHER NECESSARY EQUIPMENT AND START FILMING!

SIDESTEP

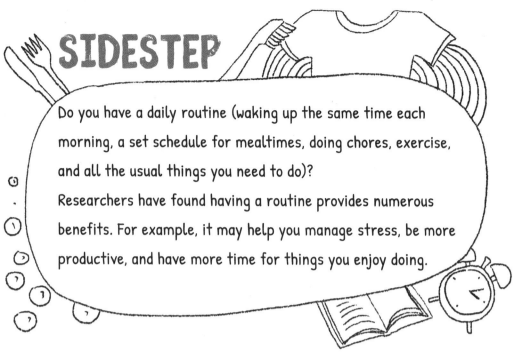

Do you have a daily routine (waking up the same time each morning, a set schedule for mealtimes, doing chores, exercise, and all the usual things you need to do)?

Researchers have found having a routine provides numerous benefits. For example, it may help you manage stress, be more productive, and have more time for things you enjoy doing.

WHAT IS YOUR DAILY ROUTINE?

Describe your typical day. If you don't have a routine, describe how you want it to look.

_____

_____

_____

_____

_____

_____

_____

_____

_____

_____

_____

_____

_____

_____

_____

_____

_____

_____

_____

Circle things which you enjoy or don't mind doing (organizing your closet, color-coding your notes, fixing things, being outside, cooking, etc.). Take notice of the kinds of activities you enjoy doing everyday.

DREAMING UP YOUR LIFE

Imagine there are absolutely NO LIMITS to what you can become or do in your life!
You can dream up anything you want to be...
a world changer, an Olympian, a YouTube star, a president... and it doesn't have to be ONE thing.

You can dream up any place you want to go, any city or town you want to live in.
Your dreams are only limited by your imagination.

So, what would your dream life be like?

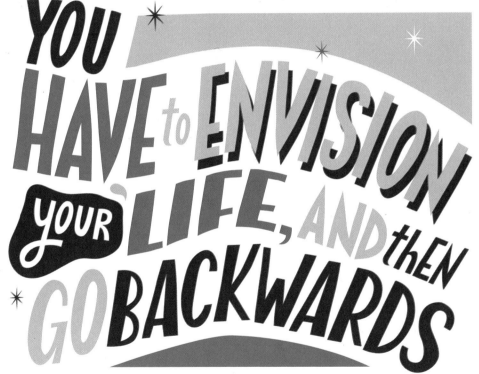

SOMEONE TOLD ME SOMETHING THAT STUCK WITH ME: YOU HAVE to ENVISION your LIFE, AND tHEN GO BACKWARDS

I'VE BEEN LIVING BY THAT MOTTO FOR A WHILE, SO I SEE WHERE I NEED TO BE. NOW I'M JUST BACKTRACKING AND TRYING TO GET BACK UP THERE.

BRUNO MARS (SINGER-SONGWRITER)

YOUR VERSION OF SUCCESS...
IT CAN BE AS UNIQUE AS YOU ARE

When we think about our goals and future, it's important to define what success means to us personally.

Sometimes we get distracted by following other successful people and thinking that if we only had what they had, we would be successful too. The reality is we all have different ideas of what success means, depending on our personalities, background, environment, and so on.

Defining what success means to YOU is one of the most important steps in creating a life that truly makes you HAPPY.

When you achieve YOUR personal version of success, you have truly won!

HOW DOES SUCCESS LOOK?

GRADUATING

HELPING OTHERS

LIVING IN A BIG CITY

BEING THE BEST AT SOMETHING

BEING ADVENTUROUS

CHANGING THE WORLD   BECOMING A DOCTOR

PURSUING EXCELLENCE

BEING ORGANIZED   FEELING LOVED

HAVING THINGS YOU WANT

LEARNING HOW TO CODE

HAVING LOTS OF FRIENDS

GETTING AN APARTMENT

BEING POPULAR

CREATING   BEING KIND

BEING INDEPENDENT

LIVING IN THE COUNTRYSIDE

GETTING A JOB   FEELING SECURE

HAVING A BIG FAMILY

BEING RICH

WHAT DOES SUCCESS MEAN TO YOU?

How do YOU define success? You can have more than one definition.
Add your own ideas below.

TO ME, SUCCESS MEANS...

BEING

FEELING

PURSUING

BECOMING

HAVING

ONE rainy afternoon an inspired 15-year old boy named **JOHN GODDARD** sat down at his kitchen table, grabbed a yellow paper pad and wrote, "My Life List." Under that heading he wrote down 127 goals.

A lot of his goals were challenging adventures like climbing the world's major mountains, exploring the longest rivers of the world and piloting the world's fastest aircraft. But he also wrote other types of goals like having a family, composing music, and teaching. John lived an exciting life full of adventures, experiences, and challenges. He had a lot of goals to accomplish and he took them very seriously!

"When I was fifteen," he once said, "all the adults I knew seemed to complain, 'Oh, if only I'd done this or that when I was younger.' They had let life slip them by. I was sure that if I planned for it, I could have a life of excitement and fun and knowledge".
John reached 109 of these quests and was once named "the modern-day Indiana Jones".

☐ Travel through the Grand Canyon on foot and by boat

☐ Learn to play polo

☐ Compose music

☐ Become proficient in the use of a plane, motorcycle, tractor, surfboard, rifle, pistol, canoe, microscope, football, basketball, bow and arrow, lariat, and boomerang

☐ Run a mile in five minutes

☐ Build own telescope

☐ Write a book

☐ Marry and have children

☐ Teach a college course

☐ Type 50 words a minute

☐ Play the flute and violin

☐ Dive in a submarine

☐ Study dragon lizards

☐ Circumnavigate the globe

☐ Visit a movie studio

☐ Learn water and snow skiing

☐ Learn jujitsu

☐ Study native medicines and bring back useful ones

☐ Publish an article in National Geographic Magazine

☐ Fly in a blimp, balloon, and glider

Mark with "x" any items on John's life list which you want to accomplish too!

BUCKET LIST

Now create your own Bucket List (or Life List) and write down everything you want to do or become.

Focus on experiences (traveling, learning how to do something, meeting certain people, etc.) rather than things because this is what makes our life more full and satisfying. Both big and small experiences matter!

Feel free to borrow ideas from other people's Bucket Lists, but remember: this list is yours.

TRAVEL

☐ _____

☐ _____

☐ _____

☐ _____

☐ _____

ADVENTURE AND FUN

☐ _____

☐ _____

☐ _____

☐ _____

☐ _____

OTHER (LEARNING, FAMILY, ETC.)

☐ _____

☐ _____

☐ _____

☐ _____

☐ _____

Pro-tip: Take a picture of this list so you can look at it at any time.

Remember to celebrate every time you check an item off your list!

Imagine the next **TEN YEARS** have passed and were the best years of your life! You're ten years older, and you're living your DREAM life. **WHAT WOULD YOUR TYPICAL DAY BE LIKE?**

Draw or write what you see in great detail, from the time you wake up until the time you fall asleep. What do you eat for breakfast? How do you spend your time and with whom? What are you doing to impact the world? This is your dream; it can be as big and wild or quiet and calm as you'd like!

8 AM

10 AM

12 PM

3 PM

5 PM

8 PM

10 PM

12 AM

You just described a perfect day of your DREAM life, ten years from now. Now, let's keep imagining...

Who have you become? What have you accomplished? What about your relationships, your health, and the things you do for fun?

IN TEN YEARS FROM NOW....

DESCRIBE WHAT YOU DO

_____

_____

_____

DESCRIBE HOW YOU FEEL

_____

_____

_____

_____

DESCRIBE YOUR FRIENDSHIPS AND RELATIONSHIPS

_____

_____

_____

LIST SKILLS YOU HAVE ACQUIRED

_____

_____

LIST THINGS YOU HAVE ACCOMPLISHED

_____

_____

_____

DESCRIBE THINGS YOU DO FOR FUN

_____

_____

NOW think about the kind of person you want to be 10 years from now. On the next page, circle or underline the qualities you would like to be known for in the future. Write your own ideas below.

NAME A PERSON WHO INSPIRES YOU OR WHO YOU WANT TO BE SIMILAR TO

WHY DID YOU CHOOSE THIS PERSON?

ORIGINAL COURAGEOUS HELPFUL PEACEFUL
RESPONSIBLE CURIOUS
WISE RESPONSIBLE POPULAR
ROMANTIC GENEROUS IMPRESSIVE
ADVENTUROUS STEADY EXTRAORDINARY
INTELLIGENT LOVABLE
CALM ORGANIZED

THE PERSON I WANT TO BE IN 10 YEARS

LOVING
TOLERANT
DECISIVE HARDWORKING
PRACTICAL DARING
PASSIONATE HEALTHY OPTIMISTIC
KIND CONFIDENT
SOCIABLE FOCUSED
SECURE AMBITIOUS

Imagine you've been invited onto the **ELLEN DEGENERES SHOW**: one of those really great ones where her kindness leads her to give something away. Remember, it's still 10 years into the future. She has chosen you to win $150,000 for your biggest achievement!

Perhaps you wrote a book that changed people's lives or invented something. Or maybe, you received an award for being courageous. Answer Ellen's questions below to tell the audience about your achievement.

TELL US WHAT YOU'VE DONE TO RECEIVE THIS AWARD.

_____

_____

_____

_____

WHAT'S ONE THING THAT KEPT YOU MOTIVATED TO ACHIEVE THIS?

_____

_____

_____

_____

Though you received a lot of money with the award, there's a catch: you can't spend it on yourself. You must use the money to help someone in need, to make something meaningful, or to help someone achieve their dreams.

HOW WOULD YOU SPEND THE MONEY?

Below, draw a comic illustrating this scenario. Include some dialogue so you'll remember just how big of a difference you made for someone.

CREATE YOUR DREAM BOARD!

A great way to dream up your future is to create a Dream (or Vision) Board. It's a place where you display images, which represent your dreams.

A Dream Board helps clearly define your dreams, plans, and goals in a visual way. It can serve as an inspiration and motivation. You can create a Dream Board for any period: a month, a year, or 5 years into the future.

Most people make a board that looks like a collage, but it can also be sketched, or made up entirely of words.

And once it's done, you can hang it in your bedroom or living room — essentially, wherever you spend a good amount of time.

You can create a `physical` Dream Board by using a poster board and pinning or gluing photos, drawings, quotes, and other images.

You can also create a `digital` Dream Board. Search for images such as places you want to visit, things you want to do, people you want to meet, etc. Organize the images and quotes with a free tool like Trello or Evernote.

Sketch or draw your Dream Board here. Use words, drawings, quotes, etc. - anything which visually represents your dreams about your future life.

IF YOU CAN BELIEVE IN SOMETHING GREAT, THEN YOU CAN ACHIEVE SOMETHING GREAT.

KATY PERRY
(SINGER-SONGWRITER)

THE SECRET TO BECOMING HAPPIER...

Usually we dream about things which would make OUR OWN lives better. However, you can think about your dreams and your future from a different perspective: how the things you do and the person you become can help others and make the world a better place.

WHY? Research in neuroscience and psychology shows by helping OTHERS you can become happier YOURSELF. You will also be more likely to stay motivated if the dream or goal you're working towards will benefit other people and the world around you.

THE HELPER'S HIGH

Psychologists have identified a typical state of euphoria reported by those engaged in helping others. They call it "helper's high," and it's based on the theory that giving produces endorphins in the brain and provide a mild version of a morphine high.

TURN "ME" DREAMS INTO "WORLD" DREAMS

Same dream, different perspective:

A "**ME**" dream: I want to become an engineer.

A "**WORLD**" dream: I want to create cool products that would make other people's lives easier.

NOW THINK ABOUT ONE OF YOUR BIGGEST DREAMS...

Write down a "ME" version of your dream (how it will benefit you):

_____

_____

_____

_____

Write down a "WORLD" version of your dream (how it will benefit other people):

_____

_____

_____

IN TIMES OF DESPAIR, YOU MAY **BELIEVE** THE CYNIC WHO TELLS THAT ONE PERSON CANNOT MAKE A DIFFERENCE AND THERE ARE TIMES IT MAY BE HARD TO SEE **YOUR OWN IMPACT.** I BEG YOU TO REMEMBER THAT IT IS NOT POSSIBLE AT THIS TIME OR ANY TIME TO KNOW THE END RESULTS OF **YOUR EFFORTS.**

EVAN SPIEGEL (SNAPCHAT FOUNDER)

Sometimes it might seem one person can't make a difference. But remember, all the world's inventions and movements started with ONE person's idea.

To change the world, you don't need grand ideas. Trust your ideas are unique and significant.

DO YOU HAVE AN IDEA THAT COULD IMPROVE THE WORLD? Perhaps it's a new app which solves a problem or an invention to make people's lives better. Write it down or sketch it below.

If you're not sure yet, that's OK! Read the story on the following page about Ann Makosinski, and her inventions, to get inspired.

IF you were asked to imagine a brilliant inventor, you would probably think of someone older than 40 and swathes of complex equipment and mind-bending equations. You might imagine James Dyson or Elon Musk...

But what if you imagined a young woman with a normal life, who likes cats and Elvis Presley, and also has an extraordinary drive for finding and solving problems?

That young woman is ANN MAKOSINSKI who was born in Victoria, Canada. Ann is one of the world's most intelligent, creative, and inspiring inventors, despite her young age.

She began inventing when she was only 7. When Ann was 15 her "Hollow Flashlight" invention was already winning awards.

The idea for her invention came about when her friend in the Philippines failed her grade because she did not have light to study at night. Ann knew this was just not good enough and there had to be a simple solution...which she was holding in the palm of her hand. Voila: a flashlight which runs from the heat of the user's hand.

Her gift of heat generated light is now on the way to helping countless students in developing areas to achieve their goals.

On a mission to help her peers yet again, Ann created the eDrink: a mug that uses the heat from hot drinks to charge a cell phone and extend the battery life for up to 30 minutes.

Ann is an example of someone who not only thinks of great ideas, but also puts them into action. Her ingenuity is what sets her apart from others and inspires all of us to think, act, and create positive change. As she said herself, "Make your own solutions, don't wait for others to do it for you."

SIDESTEP

How old will you be in **50 YEARS**? And how do you think the world will look then? Here are some questions scientists and researchers ask themselves about the future of the world. Write what YOU think.

WILL HUMANS LIVE ANYWHERE ELSE IN THE SOLAR SYSTEM BEYOND EARTH?

_____

_____

_____

_____

WHAT WILL THE ROLE OF ROBOTS BE? WILL THEY LOOK LIKE PEOPLE OR MACHINES?

_____

_____

_____

_____

WILL PEOPLE BE TRAVELING TO PLACES LIKE THEY DO
TODAY OR WILL THEY USE VIRTUAL REALITY TO SEE
THE PLACES THEY WANT TO VISIT?

_____

_____

_____

_____

_____

HOW WILL PEOPLE SPEND THEIR FREE TIME
IN THE FUTURE?

_____

_____

_____

_____

_____

The next chapter will give you tools and strategies for turning
your dreams into reality!

FROM DREAMS TO REALITY

Amazing things can happen when you start following your dreams. Your life can be filled with adventure, fun, and excitement! It might also take unexpected turns, but they can be intriguing and memorable challenges.

And more importantly, as you're following your dreams and working on your goals, YOU will change too! You will become more courageous, adaptable, and resilient.

You will become a person who inspires others to dream and achieve!

Have a dream, chase it down, jump over every single hurdle, and run through **FIRE** and **ICE** to get there.

Whitney Wolfe Herd, founder of Bumble

In the previous chapter, you imagined the life you want to have and you created your Bucket List and/or Dream Board.

Now, to transform your dreams into reality, you need to turn your dreams into a series of GOALS.

HOW?

Make a list of what you need to accomplish and what needs to happen before you start living your dream.

BREAK THAT LIST OF TO-DO'S INTO A SEQUENCE OF STEPS, ALMOST AS IF YOU WERE CLIMBING A STAIRCASE TOWARDS YOUR DREAM.

These steps are your goals.

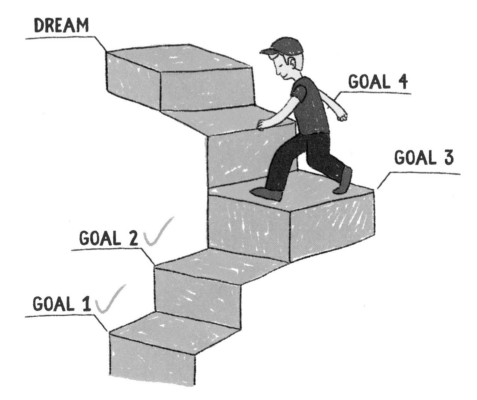

DREAM

GOAL 4

GOAL 3

GOAL 2 ✓

GOAL 1 ✓

DREAMS ARE LIKE A BLUEPRINT
PROVIDING YOU WITH THE
VISION OF WHERE YOU WANT TO
GO.

GOALS ARE THE MEANS TO
MAKE YOUR BLUEPRINT COME TO
LIFE. THEY ARE THE WORKERS
THAT HELP YOU TRANSFORM YOUR
DREAMS INTO REALITY.

LIFE WITHOUT GOALS
AIMLESSLY DRIFTING

LIFE WITH GOALS
MOVING WITH PURPOSE

IMAGINE TWO DIFFERENT KINDS OF PEOPLE...

The first person doesn't have goals. She drifts aimlessly in the sea of life and is taken away by the waves to places she never wanted to go in the first place. Eventually, she becomes complacent and unmotivated, and her life becomes dull and predictable.

The second person sets her goals and works hard towards them. She moves towards the destination she has chosen. Whether fast and furious or slow and steady, it doesn't matter. She pursues her goal with determination. This person becomes resilient, brave, and unstoppable. Her life is purposeful, adventurous, and fun. She might not reach the exact destination, but she will certainly be heading in the right direction!

WHAT KIND OF PERSON WOULD YOU LIKE TO BE?

WHAT YOU GET BY ACHIEVING YOUR GOALS IS NOT AS IMPORTANT AS WHAT YOU BECOME BY ACHIEVING YOUR GOALS.

- Zig Ziglar

NOW LET'S SET SOME GOALS!

Follow the steps below and see the example on the next page. You have two templates (the following two pages) to create GOALS and ACTIONS for your big dreams.

1. Write down YOUR DREAM at the top of the staircase (choose one or several from the previous chapter).

2. Write down your FIRST GOAL at the very bottom of the staircase. This is your first step towards your dream. Write down your FIRST ACTION towards your first goal.

3. Create your second goal and the first action towards it.

4. Create your third goal and the first action towards it.

   ...and so on! You can have more or less than three goals if you choose. It's up to you.

Writing your first action towards each goal is very powerful! It will give you a clear start and you will be more likely to start working on your goal.

DREAM: BECOME A WORLD-RENOWNED MUSICIAN

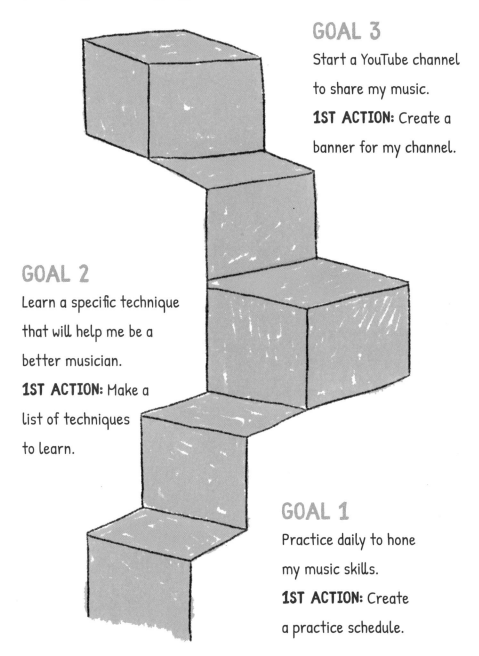

GOAL 3
Start a YouTube channel to share my music.
1ST ACTION: Create a banner for my channel.

GOAL 2
Learn a specific technique that will help me be a better musician.
1ST ACTION: Make a list of techniques to learn.

GOAL 1
Practice daily to hone my music skills.
1ST ACTION: Create a practice schedule.

YOUR DREAM: _____

GOAL 3 _____

_____

_____

1ST ACTION: _____

_____

GOAL 2 _____

_____

_____

1ST ACTION: _____

_____

_____

GOAL 1 _____

_____

_____

1ST ACTION: _____

_____

_____

YOUR DREAM: _____

GOAL 3 _____

_____

1ST ACTION: _____

_____

GOAL 2 _____

_____

1ST ACTION: _____

_____

_____

GOAL 1 _____

_____

_____

1ST ACTION: _____

You can draw similar pictures in your
notebook and do this exercise for all
the dreams you would like to pursue.

_____

_____

THE MORE SPECIFIC YOUR GOALS ARE, THE BETTER YOUR CHANCES ARE OF REACHING THEM.

So now let's bring more clarity to your goals. Take your FIRST goal from the previous page and add more details.

WRITE DOWN THE GOAL HERE:

_____

_____

_____

BY WHEN DO YOU WANT TO ACHIEVE IT (AN APPROXIMATE DATE)?

_____

HOW WILL YOU KNOW YOU HAVE ACHIEVED IT?

_____

_____

WHAT HAVE YOU ALREADY DONE TOWARDS YOUR GOAL?

_____

_____

_____

YOU CAN IMPROVE YOUR CHANCES OF REACHING YOUR GOALS BY ENVISIONING FUTURE OBSTACLES AND WAYS YOU CAN OVERCOME THEM.

Let's think about what could PREVENT you from reaching the goal you wrote about on the previous page.

What are two possible reasons you could give up? For example, you might feel distracted and begin to procrastinate. To overcome this, you could set aside a specific amount of time in your schedule to work on this goal.

REASON ONE:

_____

WHAT WILL YOU DO TO OVERCOME THIS CHALLENGE?

_____

_____

REASON TWO:

_____

WHAT WILL YOU DO TO OVERCOME THIS CHALLENGE?

_____

_____

If you're not sure how to overcome the challenges that might cause you to give up on your goal, see the NEXT chapter for ideas!

Now you have a lot of goals! How to track them all?

YOU CAN START TRACKING YOUR GOALS USING A SIMPLE TOOL LIKE THE ONE BELOW.

Alternatively, create a spreadsheet or write your goals in the notes section on your phone.

You can also find an app to track your goals. Some productivity apps like Evernote can be used in so many ways, including goal setting and tracking.

YOUR DREAMS OR BIG GOALS	BREAK IT DOWN (smaller goals or actions)	DUE DATE
achieve by:		☐ ☐ ☐ ☐
achieve by:		☐ ☐ ☐ ☐
achieve by:		☐ ☐ ☐ ☐

THERE *will* -BE- OBSTACLES

THERE *will* -BE- DOUBTERS

THERE *will* -BE- MISTAKES

BUT WITH

HARD WORK

THERE ARE

NO LIMITS

Michael Phelps, Olympic Swimmer

THE world is full of problems to be solved and dreams to be realized. For some, like **EDDA ARNADOTTIR HAMAR**, these go hand in hand.

Let's travel back in time to Edda's early years. We find a five year old girl sailing across the seas from Iceland to Australia. Along the way, she learns about our incredible world and gains true appreciation for our planet, which plants the seed for her future dream.

Fast-forward thirteen years and we find Edda experiencing the fashion world first hand at the age of 20. This experience will spark her passion for change and innovation in a world where waste is rife and landfills are brimming and spilling evermore.

She didn't just see the glamour and excitement of the fashion world, however. She looked through the haze and saw the problems hiding beneath.

The waste bothered her, and she was determined to do something about it. A new, powerful dream was born: to transform the way we produce, source and recycle clothing.

The vastness of Edda's dream didn't scare her. It spurred her on and fed the fire which fueled a series of manageable, yet significant steps.

The first step was to create a fashion show, Undress Runways, to celebrate the talented work of ethical designers from around the world. She invited creators who use organic fabrics, zero-waste collections, ethically produced garments, and recycled accessories. Eventually, Undress Runways became Australia's largest sustainable fashion runway show.

Next on her quest for change, Edda added another stepping stone. She launched an annually published magazine on the future of fashion, The Naked Mag. Her goal was to empower readers to make informed and socially conscious decisions when making purchases.

Her next step was to turn to the digital world and create an app called Lána. The app connects people all around the world who are in need of temporary clothing items as they travel and those who have the garments to offer.

Edda keeps her eyes firmly on her dream and weaves and braids her way through on a creative path towards success.

What's more remarkable is how her determination to make a difference, fueled by her skill to set and achieve goals, is helping her transform the massive and rigid fashion industry. As Edda said, "If you do the right things in the right order, you'll get there."

CREATE THE JAR OF AWESOME!

No matter how big your dream is, it's important to celebrate small wins that move you closer to it! It can make all the difference in how you feel about your progress and will help you stay motivated.

CREATE THE JAR OF AWESOME TO KEEP TRACK OF AND CELEBRATE YOUR SUCCESSES AND SMALL WINS.

STEP 1. Find an empty jar (if you can't find a jar, you can use any small container).

STEP 2. Create a label. You can use a small piece of paper (or a Post-It note) and tape it to the jar.

STEP 3. As you accomplish a goal or have a small win, write it down on a piece of paper and put in the jar.

When you contribute to your Jar of Awesome, make sure to celebrate and reflect on the whole journey!

Alternatively, you can create a success journal. Use a notebook or a blank journal where you can list your wins and accomplishments... even the smallest ones!

Pro-tip: every time you feel unmotivated or discouraged, re-read the wins from your jar or success journal. It will help you to keep going!

BELOW, WRITE DOWN TWO RECENT WINS OR GOALS YOU HAVE ACCOMPLISHED.

They are going straight into your Jar of Awesome!

THE JAR OF AWESOME

The idea of The Jar of Awesome comes from Tim Ferriss, the popular author and podcaster.

YOU CAN SKYROCKET YOURSELF TO THE TOP OF THE LADDER BY LEARNING NEW SKILLS.

When you learn the skills you need to reach your goals, your chances of success skyrocket! Think of your skills as a catapult that can get you to where you want to be.

SO... WHAT SKILLS DO YOU NEED TO ACHIEVE YOUR GOALS AND MAKE YOUR DREAMS A REALITY?

Below, CHECK off the skills you already have and CIRCLE the ones you need to learn in order to reach the goals you're currently working on. On empty rows, write any skills that are missing on the list.

THE SKILLS I NEED TO...

BE MORE PRODUCTIVE

- [ ] Managing my time effectively
- [ ] Setting and tracking goals
- [ ] Planning (my day, a project, etc.)
- [ ] Paying attention to details
- [ ] Managing my stress
- [ ] Sticking to a task
- [ ] _____
- [ ] _____

COMMUNICATE BETTER

- [ ] Presenting ideas to others
- [ ] Speaking publicly
- [ ] Meeting and getting to know new people
- [ ] Listening effectively
- [ ] Persuading others
- [ ] Expressing my needs clearly
- [ ] Managing my emotions
- [ ] _____
- [ ] _____

START A BUSINESS

- [ ] Branding
- [ ] Marketing
- [ ] Managing money
- [ ] Leading others
- [ ] Solving problems
- [ ] Working with numbers (building spreadsheets, etc.)
- [ ] Thinking from other people's perspective (empathy)

_____

_____

CREATE THINGS

- [ ] Coding
- [ ] Graphic design
- [ ] Video editing
- [ ] Photography
- [ ] Building a website

_____

_____

LIST ANY OTHER SKILLS THAT WILL CATAPULT YOU TO YOUR GOALS

- [ ] _____
- [ ] _____
- [ ] _____
- [ ] _____
- [ ] _____

Sometimes we might think we're only good at certain things. As a result, we might be limiting ourselves and setting smaller goals, which don't get us where we TRULY want to go.

The reality is you can LEARN to become good at many things. When you're learning something, you're building new connections in your brain (that's why it might feel difficult at first).

When you start practicing the thing you're learning, those connections get stronger and it becomes easier over time.

OUR BRAIN IS THAT POWERFUL AND FLEXIBLE!

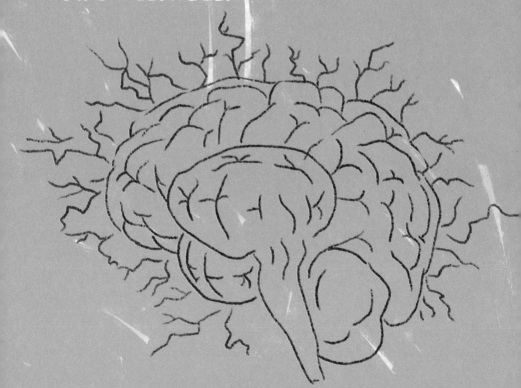

Choose two skills you want to learn from the previous pages.

NOW BRAINSTORM IDEAS TO LEARN THEM.

For example, you could take a class, find a person who has the skill and learn from them, research opportunities to practice the skill, read a blog on this topic, follow experts on social media, etc.

Write down your ideas in bullet points below.

SKILL 1: _____

THINGS I CAN DO TO LEARN IT:

- _____
- _____
- _____
- _____

SKILL 2: _____

THINGS I CAN DO TO LEARN IT:

- _____
- _____
- _____
- _____

Sometimes you might feel overwhelmed with everything you have to do each day. So when are you supposed to work on your dreams and goals? This fun exercise can help you find time in your day.

Below are 24 hours of your typical day. First, for each hour, identify your energy levels by coloring in the batteries (low energy - low charge, etc.). Second, write down your **ROUTINE ACTIVITIES** like sleeping, showering, eating, etc. in squares depending on what time you do them. Third, write down activities you do **FOR FUN** like watching videos, texting, etc.

The empty squares represent your productive time. Now think how you can increase your productive time. Circle "for fun" or non-essential activities that can be eliminated or reduced in time.

6am	7am	8am
9am	10am	11am
12am	1pm	2pm

3pm	4pm	5pm
6pm	7pm	8pm
9pm	10pm	11pm
12pm	1am	2am
3am	4am	5am

Notice the energy levels during your productive times. Can you move your schedule around so your productive time falls into your high energy hours?

YOU CAN INCREASE THE ODDS OF REACHING YOUR GOALS WITH THIS SIMPLE TRICK!

Did you know you can significantly increase the chances of reaching a goal by telling other people about it? Specifically, for this trick to work, you need to:

1. **TELL OTHER PEOPLE (OR A PERSON) ABOUT YOUR GOAL**
2. **SHARE WHY YOU WANT TO ACHIEVE IT**
3. **REPORT BACK ON YOUR PROGRESS (REGULARLY)**

This works because you begin to feel accountable to someone for doing what you said you would do. As a result, you feel more motivated to keep going!

Let's practice! Think of a goal you're currently working on (e.g., a bad habit you want to get rid of). **WHAT IS IT?**

_____

_____

WHY DO YOU WANT TO ACHIEVE THIS GOAL?

_____

_____

• Now share your answers with either a trusted friend OR post about it on social media. Notice how you feel once you do that.
• Remember to regularly check back with the people with whom you shared, and tell them about your progress towards this goal.

I'M CONTINUALLY TRYING TO MAKE CHOICES THAT PUT ME AGAINST MY OWN COMFORT ZONE. AS LONG AS YOU'RE UNCOMFORTABLE, IT MEANS YOU'RE GROWING.

ASHTON KUTCHER, ACTOR

AS we move through life we are presented with doors that lead to bright opportunities. Some open easily and some must be forced open with sheer determination. And sometimes even tightly locked doors can be opened with the help of others.

VICKY ROY was born into a world of uncertainty and hardship. As a young boy in West Bengal, he suffered at the hands of violence from which he fled at the age of eleven. He joined the many other children who begged, worked, and cheated affliction to survive on the busy streets of New Delhi.

Vicky Roy's life took a fortunate turn when he was welcomed into the care of the Salaam Baalak Trust, where street children are taken in and nurtured. It was there Roy discovered his true calling; a calling which consumed him and filled him with passion. He learned about photography and the power of telling stories through images.

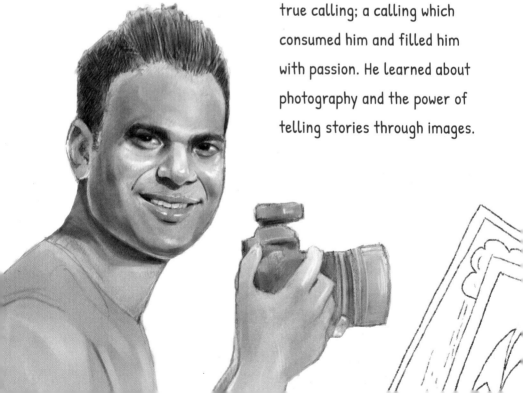

Under the wing of his first mentor, Dixcy Benjamin, Roy soaked up all the knowledge generously offered to him. Roy found great motivation through a simple piece of advice: "The more pictures you take, the better you will get."

Once he ventured from the Trust and out into the world as a thriving eighteen year old man, Roy accepted the help of another mentor, a Delhi-based photographer named Annieman.

Under Annieman's guiding hand, Roy opened his first exhibition, "Street Dreams". It was a collection of photographs that took the observer on a journey through the life of street children. Roy's exhibition captured the hearts and imaginations of those who viewed it, and its success was colossal.

"Street Dreams" saw Roy bursting through many doors. He became the winner of a photography competition and went to the USA to study his craft in the world's best photography school.

Now Vicky Roy is a world-renowned photographer with many international photography projects under his belt. He attributes much of his success to the people who gave him their time and knowledge, fostered and nurtured his talent, and supported his burning passion.

HAVING THE SUPPORT OF OTHERS GREATLY INCREASES YOUR CHANCES OF SUCCESS.

Many, if not all, successful people received a lot of help from others before they became successful. It's very difficult - almost impossible - to accomplish great things alone!

To achieve your goals, you will also need advice, help, and feedback from other people. This can be someone you already know or someone you don't personally know yet but get inspired by, and would like to meet one day.

List the names of people YOU ALREADY KNOW who you can reach out to for help.

List the names of people **YOU DON'T YET KNOW** (e.g., global experts or people in your community) who you can reach out to for help.

_____

_____

_____

_____

_____

_____

TAKE ON THIS CHALLENGE!

Choose one person from the two lists you just created and circle their name. Within the next 3 days, **REACH OUT** to this person and ask for their help or advice on something you're currently struggling with.

Pro- tip: when you ask for help, make sure to offer something of value in return (e.g., your time, your skills, anything else this person might benefit from). If you're not sure what to offer, ask them how you can be helpful.

SIDESTEP

Habits are such an integral part of your daily life. Almost everything you do revolves around habits.

Some habits can prevent us from reaching our goals. For example, if you have a habit of arriving late, you might miss a lot of important opportunities.

By learning how to develop better habits to replace bad habits, you will be able to set yourself up for success.

WHAT BAD HABITS DO YOU WANT TO BREAK?

_____

_____

_____

_____

_____

_____

WHAT NEW HABITS DO YOU WANT TO LEARN?

Check the ones you would like to learn below.

- [ ] Plan your day
- [ ] Set goals
- [ ] Get up early
- [ ] Save money
- [ ] Arrive early to meetings / appointments
- [ ] Organize your workspace
- [ ] Manage your time effectively
- [ ] Drink water
- [ ] Exercise regularly
- [ ] Eat healthy
- [ ] Meditate
- [ ] Get enough sleep
- [ ] Walk or bike to places
- [ ] Take vitamins
- [ ] Make your bed
- [ ] Read books
- [ ] Practice affirmations
- [ ] Perform regular acts of kindness
- [ ] Journal your thoughts
- [ ] _____
- [ ] _____
- [ ] _____

THE KEY TO SUCCESS

When you are chasing your dreams, be prepared to face obstacles and possibly even fail.

Every dreamer who dares to chase their dreams goes through challenging times. Those dreamers who don't let detours stop them are the ones who win! As they persevere, they get better and stronger.

Remember, challenges and failures are just the stepping stones on the path to your dreams!

the STRUGGLES
I'M FACING
THE CHANCES
I'M TAKING
SOMETIMES MIGHT
KNOCK ME DOWN
BUT NO
I'M NOT BREAKING

Miley Cyrus, *singer-songwriter*

THE MOST IMPORTANT REASON WHY YOU SHOULD NOT QUIT OR GIVE UP:

Sometimes you might feel unmotivated and want to quit what you're working on instead of continuing. You might think, "What's the point?" or "Why keep trying?"

Here's the thing...there's a BIG downside to quitting. When we quit something, our brain literally rewires itself so it's easier for us to quit in the future. It's incredible how adaptable our brain is!

So after you quit the first time, the next time you find yourself in a challenging situation, you will be more likely to surrender instead of tackling the challenge. Quitting, like persisting, becomes a habit.

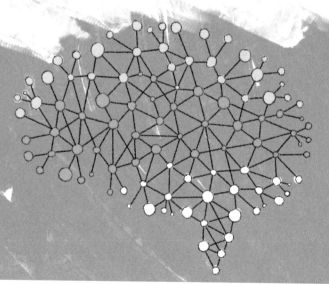

"The first time you quit, it's hard. The second time, it gets easier. The third time, you don't even have to think about it."
– **BEAR BRYANT**, college football coach

WHEN QUITTING IS AN OPTION

Now, there are times when quitting might actually be the right choice.
For example, when the thing you're working on was not a good idea in
the first place, it makes sense to stop.

Unfortunately, there are no definitive guidelines on when to give up and
when to keep trying. There are some questions, however, that can help
you make the decision.

THINK ABOUT SOMETHING YOU'RE CONSIDERING QUITTING. WHAT IS IT?

_____

_____

BY QUITTING, WHAT OPPORTUNITY WILL YOU MISS?

_____

_____

BY QUITTING, WHAT MIGHT YOU LATER REGRET?

_____

_____

If missed opportunities and potential regrets are too big, perhaps
continuing is the right choice.

WHEN YOU FEEL LIKE IT'S TOO MUCH...

Sometimes when you're working on something challenging, you might want to quit quite simply because you're tired and overwhelmed. In those moments, it helps to take a moment and reflect.

To determine if you need to take a break or try something different, ask yourself the following questions:

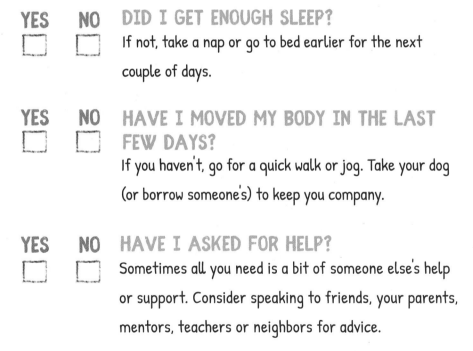

YES **NO** **DID I GET ENOUGH SLEEP?**
☐ ☐ If not, take a nap or go to bed earlier for the next couple of days.

YES **NO** **HAVE I MOVED MY BODY IN THE LAST FEW DAYS?**
☐ ☐ If you haven't, go for a quick walk or jog. Take your dog (or borrow someone's) to keep you company.

YES **NO** **HAVE I ASKED FOR HELP?**
☐ ☐ Sometimes all you need is a bit of someone else's help or support. Consider speaking to friends, your parents, mentors, teachers or neighbors for advice.

Notice if you feel less overwhelmed after you have tried some of these things. Are there any other things you can try to feel better and less overwhelmed?

When you feel stressed and overwhelmed, it might help to take a 5-10 minute break and do something else. Below, circle things you can try the next time you need a short break.

Pro-tip: if you want your break to be REALLY effective, put your phone somewhere where you can't easily reach it (like the top of your fridge).

"I'M FINDING IT DIFFICULT TO CONCENTRATE BUT I'M NOT SURE WHY..."

DO YOU KEEP PUTTING THINGS OFF?

Sometimes the biggest challenge is to take action. When procrastination takes over we get sidetracked and nothing gets done. We find excuses for why today is not the right day to accomplish our goals.

THINK ABOUT THE GOAL YOU'RE PUTTING OFF. WHAT IS IT?

_____

_____

Now answer these questions to find reasons why you might be procrastinating.

YES   NO   IS MY GOAL TOO VAGUE?
☐   ☐   Sometimes when a goal is too vague, it's not clear what to do. A vague goal would be "to exercise". A concrete goal would be "to train for next summer's half marathon".

YES   NO   IS MY GOAL TOO GRAND?
☐   ☐   When your goal is too big it might feel overwhelming. Break the goal down into smaller steps (see chapter 4).

YES   NO   HAVE I TRIED A DIFFERENT APPROACH?
☐   ☐   When something doesn't work right away, we might get discouraged and stop trying. Brainstorm ideas on how else you can tackle the problem. Ask others for input. Try lots of things!

3 TIPS TO FINISH WHAT YOU STARTED

Set aside a specific amount of time to work on ONE thing. Set an alarm on your phone and work on this thing only. To take a break, set another alarm for 5 minutes. Alternate your work and your breaks until you get it done.

Have an Accountability Partner who will make sure you follow through till the end. Even better, agree if you don't follow through, you will owe them something in return (this alone might keep you motivated).

Find others who are working on something hard and start encouraging them to keep going. Your own attitude will improve and you will able to dive back into the work with a renewed sense of purpose.

WRITE DOWN OTHER IDEAS BELOW

WHEN YOU CAN'T
CONTROL WHAT'S
happening,
CONTROL THE WAY
you respond
TO WHAT'S HAPPENING
FOR THAT IS WHERE
your power is!

When things don't work out the way we planned or don't go our way, we might stress out and give up. There are things, however, we CAN'T actually control (e.g., other people's actions, deadlines, who your family is, etc.), so there's no point in stressing about them.

When you focus on things you CAN control (e.g., your actions, effort, attitude, etc.), life becomes simpler and more manageable.

IN THE CIRCLES BELOW, WRITE DOWN THINGS YOU CAN AND CAN'T CONTROL.

When it's **TOUGH** will you **give up,** or will you be **RELENTLESS** **?**

Jeff Bezos,
Amazon Founder

HAVE YOU EVER WRITTEN A LETTER TO YOUR YOUNGER SELF?

How old were you three years ago? You certainly accomplished and learned a lot since then. And you have a lot more experience under your belt.

THINK OF THE HARDEST THING YOU'VE DONE WITHIN THE LAST THREE YEARS — THE TIME WHEN YOU PERSEVERED AND DID NOT GIVE UP WHEN IT WAS DIFFICULT.

Perhaps, it was mastering a hard math module or a cool trick on your skateboard.

Now write a letter to your younger self and tell this story. Give yourself credit for sticking to it and if you want, give some advice on what you could have done differently.

ACCEPT YOUR FAILURES AS NECESSARY PARTS IN YOUR QUEST TO DO AND BE SOMETHING GREAT!

Sometimes we might want to quit because we're afraid to fail or make a mistake. The truth is, struggle and failure are the very ingredients of growth and success.

Think about success as an ICEBERG. Most people see the top part, but there are a lot of things which make up success and are often invisible to the outside world: failures, mistakes, challenges, and rejections.

Use the free space to write down other things below the surface which make up success.

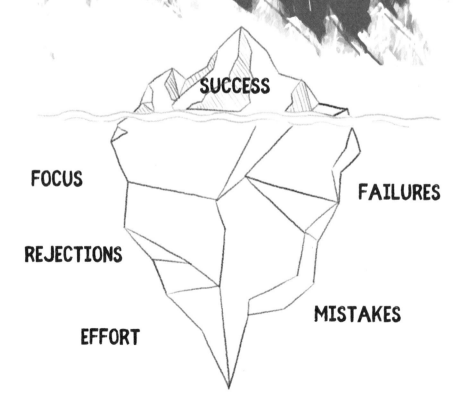

SUCCESS

FOCUS

FAILURES

REJECTIONS

MISTAKES

EFFORT

I've missed more than 9,000 shots in my career. I've lost almost 300 games. Twenty-six times I've been trusted to take the game-winning shots and <u>missed.</u> I've failed over and over and over again in my life. And that is why I SUCCEED.

Michael Jordan - basketball player

IT'S interesting how something we fear so vehemently is the very thing which can catapult us to success. Failure, setbacks and obstacles seem daunting and threaten to derail us and fling us far from the path we carved out. However, they just can't be avoided.

Failure comes knocking, even on the doors of the most clever thinkers. When failure approaches, obstacles arise, the stars don't align, and the road is blocked. There are two options: turn around, go back, and never venture out again or keep pushing forward on an unknown track.

The founders of Musical.ly, **ALEX ZHU** and **LUYU YANG**, poured their hearts, souls, time, and money into an education app called Cicada, long before Musical.ly was born.

The app was a great idea! It provided a platform where people could learn from experts who post short tutorials. But the end result came with a swathe of issues, ultimately ending in one big failure.

Instead of throwing in the towel and returning the money to the investors, Zhu took inspiration from the world around him to find a new idea.

He observed the fun, creativity, and affinity teenagers in his city had with music. From this spark came the flame of Musical.ly, a free app that allows people to create their own short music videos.

Musical.ly set out at a crawl, then a walk, then a run, and finally a sprint. The slower steps at the beginning became an advantage as it gave the team time and understanding to make the necessary changes.

These changes propelled the app into the history books of modern social technology. Now, their creation has hundreds of millions of followers and is a household name among the younger generations.

The Musical.ly founders took their initial failure as a push to open their minds and find a new niche — to find a gap which needed to be filled in the world of technology, youth, and fun.

As Zhu said, "Sometimes quick failure, like that education app, is good because you can turn around other ideas quickly."

Failing at something never makes people themselves a failure; it makes them experimenters, risk-takers, and ultimately achievers.

I WAS BORN
TO MAKE ~~THEM~~ ✓
MISTAKES,
NOT TO FAKE
~~PERFECTION.~~

DRAKE, SINGER-SONGWRITER

WHEN YOU MAKE A MISTAKE...YOUR BRAIN GROWS!

Did you know there is electrochemical activity in our brains that can ONLY happen when we make a mistake?

In fact, when you get something right, your brain does NOT grow! When you make a mistake, you struggle and have to think harder. This is when your brain grows the most.

THAT IS WHY IT IS IMPORTANT TO WORK ON HARD AND CHALLENGING PROBLEMS SO YOU CAN STRUGGLE AND MAKE MISTAKES.

BY MAKING A MISTAKE YOU ARE ACTIVELY CAUSING YOUR BRAIN TO SPARK AND GROW!

REFLECT ON YOUR FAILURES AND MISTAKES AS THEY CAN TEACH YOU POWERFUL LESSONS.

When we learn from our failures, we propel ourselves forward with more experience and knowledge to do better next time.

Think of something that didn't go your way — perhaps a big mistake or failure. Describe what happened.

_____

_____

_____

_____

WHAT HAVE YOU LEARNED FROM IT?

_____

_____

_____

_____

WHAT COULD YOU DO DIFFERENTLY NEXT TIME TO AVOID A SIMILAR MISTAKE IN THE FUTURE?

_____

_____

_____

_____

WHEN we learn about people's incredible achievements and successes, we don't often see "behind the scenes". We see the victorious end result, but we don't see all the times they tried, failed, and tried again.

AOIBHEANN O'BRIEN and **ISEULT WARD**, two entrepreneurs from Ireland, know a thing or two about journeying through failures, trials, uncertainty, and low points on the way to success.

A few years ago they became alarmed by a huge disparity in their community and the world at large: so many people were in need of food while so many businesses (like restaurants and supermarkets) were wasting perfectly good food.

They were determined to do something about it. So they founded FoodCloud, an app which connects businesses that have too much food with charities that don't have enough to feed people.

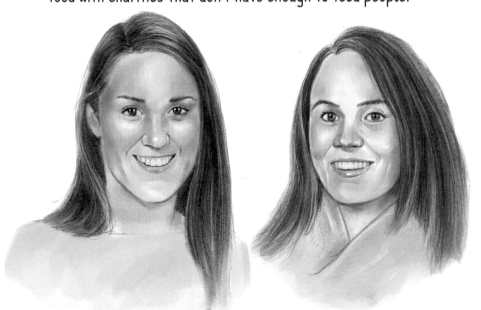

Businesses use the app to upload details of their excess food. A text goes out to local charities, who in turn pick up the donation and share it with those in need.

Unfortunately, when O'Brien and Ward first launched FoodCloud it didn't go as planned. The original model wasn't set up properly: the businesses (local bakeries and cafes) couldn't keep up with the demand and the charities didn't want to drive around Dublin to collect the food from multiple places.

Even though success seemed like a mere glimmer in the distance, O'Brien and Ward did not give up. They transformed their failure into fuel and used it to propel them toward the next step. As Iseult Ward said, "We've made loads of mistakes but it's in those moments when you reflect on what you've done wrong that the learning takes place."

To fix the problem, O'Brien and Ward reached out to supermarkets with the greatest source of excess food to meet the demand. They were able to secure strong relationships with global retailers like Aldi and Tesco and make a huge difference for the charities in their community.

There were a lot more challenges along the way, and over time, O'Brien and Ward developed a coping mechanism to utilize whenever times got tough. They thought of all the people they were helping and considered the bigger picture, both of which motivated them to keep pushing forward with their heads held high.

THE ONLY PERSON YOU SHOULD COMPARE YOURSELF TO IS THE PERSON THAT YOU WERE YESTERDAY

As you're working on your goals, you might compare yourself to others who are moving faster than you or already have what you want.

Unless you get motivated by this type of comparison, it's usually unproductive to pay attention to anyone's progress but yours.

More importantly, consider how it makes you feel when you compare yourself to others.

WHEN I COMPARE MYSELF TO OTHERS, I FEEL

_____

_____

_____

WHEN I FOCUS ON MY OWN PROGRESS, I FEEL

_____

_____

_____

SIDESTEP

WHAT IS THE BIGGEST CHANGE YOU WANT TO MAKE IN YOUR LIFE?

_____

_____

_____

_____

WHY DO YOU WANT THIS CHANGE?

_____

_____

_____

WHAT WILL IT TAKE FOR YOU TO DO IT?

_____

_____

_____

_____

Write one of your favorite quotes here — the one which inspires and motivates you.

Save this quote as a background image on your phone, it might help you in difficult times or when you need a positivity boost.

NOTES

NOTES

NOTES

NOTES

Written by Alexandra Eidens. **Design and illustrations by** Emilia Jesenska. **Quote design by** Andrea Facenda and Laetitia Ge. **Illustrations** by Sarah Saiyara and Alex Chepelev.

We would like to thank Stefanie Faye Frank and Chase Mielke for their guidance as well as our extended review and editing team.

Special thanks to Dr. Carol Dweck for her body of work on growth mindset theory.